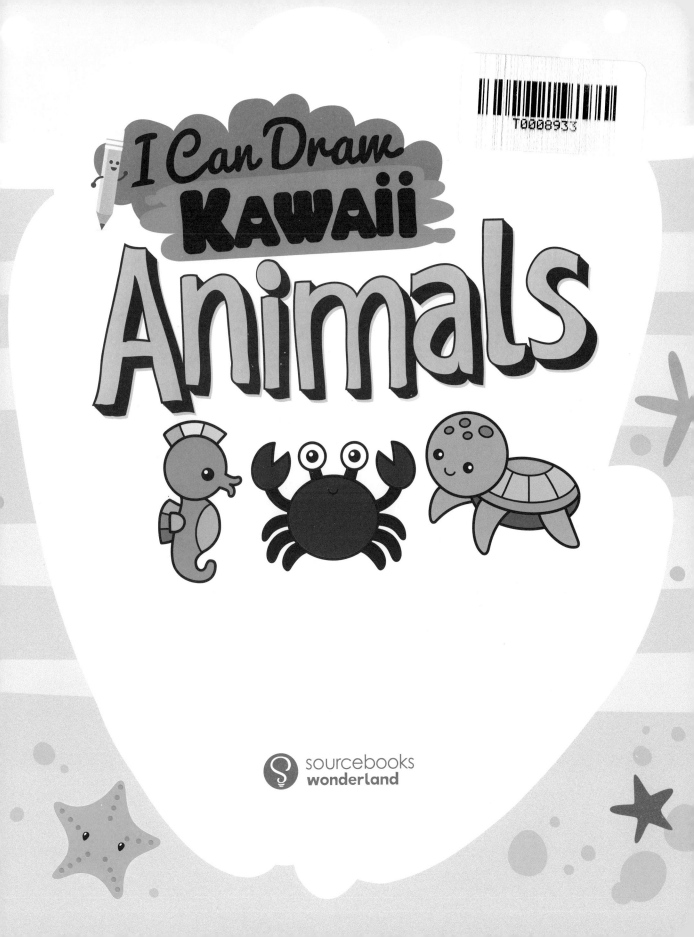

I Can Draw KAWAII Animals

sourcebooks
wonderland

Copyright © Green Android Ltd, 2022
Illustrations by Ksenya Savva
Additional illustrations courtesy of www.dreamstime.com

First edition for the United States and Canada published by:
Sourcebooks Wonderland, an imprint of Sourcebooks Kids
P.O. Box 4410, Naperville, Illinois 60567-4410
(630) 961-3900
sourcebookskids.com

The art was first sketched, then painted digitally with brushes designed by the artist.

Library of Congress Cataloging-in-Publication Data is on file with the publisher.

Source of Production: WKT Company Limited, Hong Kong
Date of Production: August 2022
Run Number: 001

Printed and bound in China.
HH 10 9 8 7 6 5 4 3 2 1

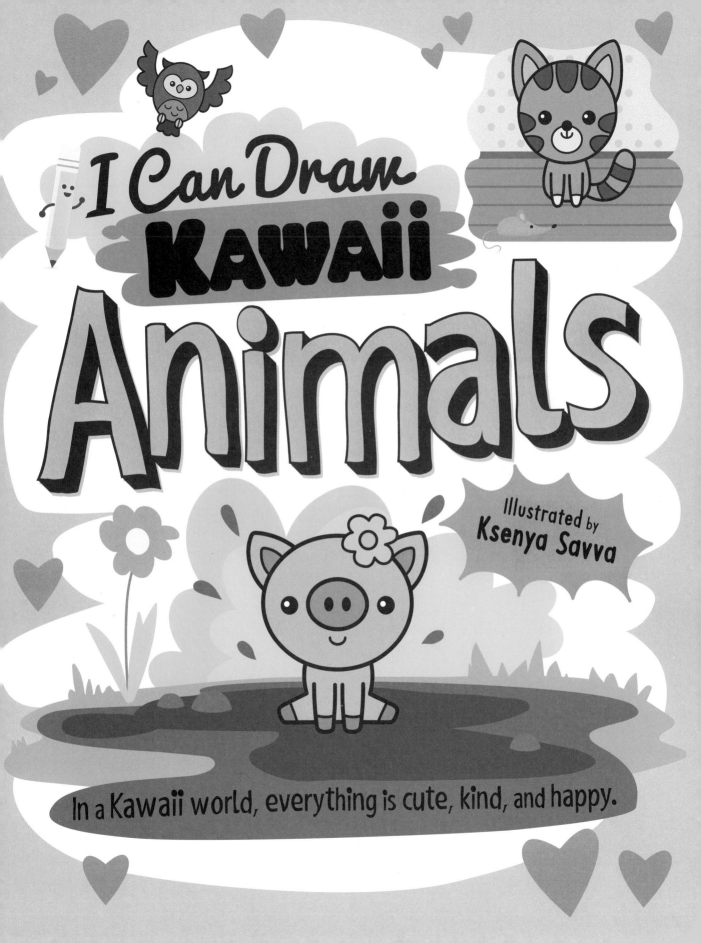

I Can Draw KAWAii Animals

Illustrated by **Ksenya Savva**

In a Kawaii world, everything is cute, kind, and happy.

What's inside this Kawaii wonderland?

18 Little green turtle

20 Splendid giraffe

22 Playful puppy

24 Cute kitten

26 Mischievous raccoon

38 Rainbow seahorse

40 Juggling octopus

42 Spouting whale

44 Snappy crab

46 Midnight flier

58 Pretty pig

60 Perfect pony

62 Adorable hippo

Which Kawaii animal are you going to draw now?

What you need

The tools needed for *I CAN DRAW KAWAII* are few and you are bound to have them all.

drawing pencil

eraser

pencil sharpener

coloring pencils or marker pens

white paper so you can draw all your favorite Kawaii animals again and again

How to draw cute Kawaii animals

Work through the five easy steps, starting with number 1.
Each step is made up of lines or simple shapes. Take your time and
don't press heavily on the pencil—pale lines are easier to erase.

1.

Make your drawing
on the practice
page the same
size as here.

2.

Only draw
what is shown
in black lines.

3.

Gray lines show
what you have
drawn in
previous steps.

4.

Gray dots
indicate lines
to be rubbed
out with
the eraser.

5.

Look closely
when drawing
small details.

Here is a finished Kawaii
animal. Follow this when
coloring your drawing.

When you have finished
your drawing and you are
happy with it, you can
go over the outlines in
black before coloring.

Don't forget to
read the idea
bubble on the
practice page.

Party-time narwhal

The narwhal with its unusual tusk is called the unicorn of the sea.
With its balloons, this narwhal is now dreamily adorable.

1.

2. draw the tusk

3. erase — add small fins

4. erase — add tail fin

5. add party balloons

draw your narwhal

Decorate this underwater party with balloons, streamers and a garland.

Squeaky mouse

If there is a mouse about, you'll hear its song-like squeaks as it tells other mice where food—and the cat—is to be found.

1.

2.

draw two big circles for ears

3.

erase

4.

5.

erase

add a long tail

and a piece of cheese

10

draw your mouse

Mice get lonely—they love company. Give squeaky mouse a best friend or two to play with.

Baby elephant

A baby elephant calf needs its mother's love and care for up to five years. The emotional bond between mother and calf is very strong.

1.

2. draw two leg shapes

draw two ovals

3. erase

4. a long trunk

5. add a flower

erase

finish the hind legs

draw your
elephant

Baby elephants love
to eat flowers. Draw
the naughty but cute
elephant a lot of
flowers to eat.

13

Terrific toucan

The toucan is known for its huge colorful and striped beak.
It lives in the lush tropical forests of South America.

1.

2.

draw a
branch

3.

top of the
huge beak

4.

erase
dotted
lines

5.

erase

14

draw your toucan

A toucan's favorite fruit are figs, guavas, and oranges. Draw trees loaded with these fruits.

Lovable llama

No one can resist a gentle, and totally huggable, llama.
It's a magical animal that makes people happy.

1.

draw a
circle
and an
oval

2.

erase

3.

finish the legs

4.

make fur
shaggy

erase

5.

draw your
Llama

Draw prickly cactus
plants covered with
colorful springtime
flowers.

17

Little green turtle

This turtle hatchling is just two inches long when it heads into the sea. It will grow to four feet in length.

2. draw an oval

3. erase · draw lines inside oval

4. add three flippers

5. add shell markings · erase

18

draw your
turtle

Turtles share their
seagrass home with
starfish, mollusks,
fish, and seahorses.
Draw the seagrass
and its animals.

Splendid giraffe

An animal that stands so tall on its long legs with its head held proudly on a long neck really deserves to be called splendid.

1. draw a circle and an oval like here

2.

3. add short horns

erase

4. there's a fluffy tip on the tail

5. don't forget the unique spots

20

draw your
giraffe

Draw a towering
leafy tree
for your
splendid giraffe.

Playful puppy

Puppies will chase a ball and wrestle stuffed toys all day.
Only when totally exhausted will they slow down and nap.

1.

2. ears at attention

3. draw an oval for the muzzle

4. half circles for hind legs   erase

5. cute nose and mouth

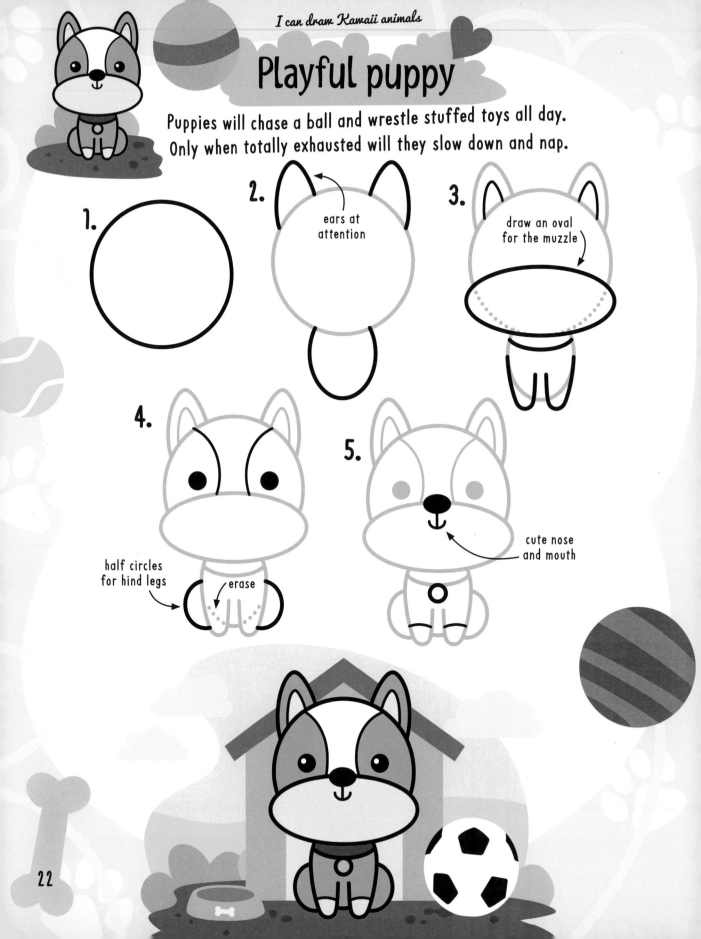

draw your
puppy

Draw balls for
your puppy to
fetch and squeaky
toys to keep
him amused.

Cute kitten

It's wonderful when a kitten curls on your lap and purrs away.
Treasure this moment—kittens are restless animals.

1.

2. draw pointy ears

3. two front legs

4. add a long swishing tail

erase

5. tabby markings

CATS
MAKE ME
HAPPY

24

draw your kitten

Kittens like to climb. Draw a climbing tower with a scratching pole, hidey-hole, toys, and a sleep hammock.

Mischievous raccoon

Racoons have long nimble fingers and nails and can open things they shouldn't. Their mischievous reputation is well deserved.

1.

2.

draw
three ovals

3.

erase

4.

erase

add a long
bushy tail

5.

don't forget
the stripes

draw your raccoon

This raccoon has prised the lid from a trash can. Draw him surrounded by food scraps and packaging.

27

Cuddly koala

Koalas are like sloths—they like to sleep. They can curl
up in the fork of a tree and snooze for 22 hours in a day.

1.

2.

draw
an oval
here

3.

make ears
furry

erase

4.

add the
nose

erase

5.

draw your
koala

Draw your koala
sitting in a tree.
Make sure there
are a lot of leaves
within reach.

29

Hungry monkey

When a monkey is moving high in the treetops, it can grip branches with both hands, both feet, and its tail.

1.

2.

draw a tilted oval

3.

erase all dotted lines

4.

5.

add the long tail

must-have banana

draw your monkey

Monkeys eat more than bananas. Draw these other monkey foods: nuts, seeds, flowers, insects, and spiders.

Snoozing panda

Should you ever meet a panda, it will lower its head or cover its face with both paws. They like to be left alone.

1.

2. draw two circles and one oval

3. erase

4. draw a small round tail

5. panda's bamboo snack

draw your
panda

zzZ

Pandas nap between
meals, often nodding
off on the forest
floor. Give panda a
cozy, leaf strewn
place to sleep.

33

Cool penguin

Penguins spend half their lives on land and half in water.
They can't fly, but boy can they dive and swim!

1.

draw
an oval

2.

draw
curved
line

3.

draw another
curved line

fish for
dinner

4.

5.

erase

34

draw your penguin

Some penguins live in freezing cold places. Draw a lot of snowflakes. Don't forget that every snowflake is different.

35

Woodland snail

Snails can eat anything, from leaves and worms to other snails!
No need to draw this snail quickly. He isn't going anywhere fast.

add eye stalks

1.

2.

draw
snail's
body

3.

a leaf for
snail to eat

draw the spiral
on the shell

4.

add a wavy
line for
the stem

5.

36

draw your snail

Draw minibeasts and creepy crawlers, like ladybugs, worms, and beetles, to keep the snail company.

Rainbow seahorse

The seahorse got its name from its long, downward pointing snout. It changes color to fit in with where it is living.

1.

2.

draw the coronet

3.

add the rest of the body

erase

4.

erase

draw two fins

5.

erase

draw your
seahorse

This seahorse lives among coral reefs. Draw colorful corals and little reef fish.

Juggling octopus

Have you ever seen an octopus juggle muffins?
No? Then you're in for a special treat with this project.

1.

2.

draw four
arms

3.

draw four
muffin tops

draw two
more arms

4.

add the
muffin
bases

5.

add yummy
chocolate
chips

40

draw your
octopus

Draw other sweet
treats like cupcakes,
candy, and donuts
for the octopus
to juggle.

Spouting whale

Whales sing using whistles, woops, and groans. A lot of people
listen to whale song recordings because they are very relaxing.

1. draw a circle

2. erase / finish the body

3. add the tail flukes

4. erase

5. add the spout of water

42

draw your whale

Whales are some of the world's largest animals. Draw other ocean giants like a manta ray and a spider crab.

Snappy crab

Snap, snap, snap go the crab's shiny claws. It uses its claw to catch food and to wave at other crabs.

2. ovals for claws — circles for eyes

3. join eyes to body — erase — join claws to body

1. draw a squashed circle

4. add walking legs

5. huge eyes

44

draw your crab

Decorate snappy crab with seashells, seaweed, anemones, and sponges. Crabs do this to hide from predators.

Midnight flier

Owls have excellent hearing and night sight. They are the only bird whose flight is totally silent. Shh! Is that an owl hooting?

1. draw a slightly tilted oval

2. huge circular eyes

3. erase

outline the wings

4. feather wing edges

a lot to erase here

5.

draw your owl

Draw your owl flying through a forest, and include the moon and a spooky bat.

Nectar collector

Bees really are busy. They will forage for nectar and pollen from trees and flowers from sunrise until sundown.

1. draw an oval

2. draw two more ovals

3. erase

4. add antenna tips — add stripes

5. finish the antennae — erase

draw your bee

A bee can't collect nectar if there are no flowers. Draw flowers and plants for the buzzing bee.

Smiley crocodile

Crocodiles can't shed tears, but they can crack a toothy grin.
But don't be fooled—it's not a friendly smile.

1. draw an oval

2. circles for eyes

3. erase — add two legs

4. erase

5. add some teeth

draw your crocodile

Some crocodiles live in ponds covered with lily pads and flowers. Add hovering dragonflies.

Colorful chameleon

To control body temperature, a chameleon changes its
skin color: light to cool down and dark to warm up.

1.

draw an
oval

2.

erase
dotted
lines

add a
curly tail

3.

draw a
branch

4.

erase

5.

add a leg
here

draw your chameleon

Draw a beetle crawling on a branch. To catch it, the chameleon will unfurl its long, sticky tongue.

Nutty squirrel

This squirrel is squireling away nuts and seeds to eat over winter.
He will dig a hole, bury the food, and carefully cover it.

1.

2. draw
rounded
triangles

3. erase

4. add a long,
bushy tail

erase

start to
draw the
acorn

5.

draw your squirrel

Squirrels love nuts, seeds, conifer cones, fruit, mushrooms, and green plants. Draw a squirrel feast.

Sleepy sloth

The adorable sloth has the cutest face and is the planet's most chilled animal. It can sleep 20 hours a day.

1. draw a tilted oval

2.

3. smaller oval inside the larger one

4. erase — add long claws

5. erase dotted lines

draw your
sloth

Fill the page
around sleepy sloth
with colorful
snoozy Zzzs in
different designs.

Pretty pig

Pigs are very smart—loads smarter than dogs—and like nothing more than putting their snout into everything.

1.

2. draw a pair of perky ears

3.

add a flower

4. add front legs

triangle shape here   erase

5.

draw your
pig

Pigs adore a good
mud bath. Draw
your pig in the
middle of a huge
muddy puddle.

Perfect pony

Imagine the most beautiful pony in the world. Her coat is shiny and smooth, and her mane and tail are a rainbow of colors.

1.

2.

3. erase

draw a long tail

4. finish the mane

erase

5.

mark hooves on legs

60

draw your pony

A special pony like this one needs an equally special crown. Draw one on her head.

Adorable hippo

Hippos live in groups with up to 30 other hippos. While adults protect the young calves, the calves just want to play, swim, and feed.

1.

2.

3.

erase

triangle
shape here

4.

erase

5.

add nostrils
and mouth

62

draw your hippo

This hippo is every hippo's best friend. Draw a pattern of colorful hearts around him.

Use this space to redraw some of your favorite animals.

Woof, please draw me again!

Meow, and me!

Neigh, and me too!